Best wishes from

Henri

HOW TO UNDERSTAND AND USE A NORWEGIAN

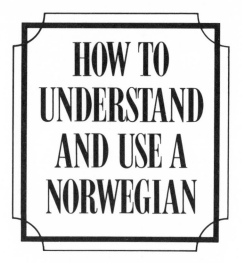

HOW TO UNDERSTAND AND USE A NORWEGIAN

A user's manual
and trouble-shooter's guide

ODD BØRRETZEN

Translated by Pat Shaw

CAPPELEN

© J.W.Cappelens Forlag a.s, Oslo 2003

Originalens tittel: Hvordan forstå og bruke en nordmann.
En bruksanvisning med feilsøkingsskjema

Illustrasjoner: Odd Børretzen
Omslagsdesign: Alex Wisting
Oversatt av Pat Shaw
Trykt hos Gjøvik Trykkeri A.s, 2003

Denne boken finnes også i norsk utgave

This book comes also in a Norwegian edition
Translated from Norwegian by Pat Shaw
Cover design: Alex Wisting
Printed in Gjøvik Trykkeri A.s, Norway 2003

ISBN 82-02-23019-5

Denne boken er tidligere utgitt av Aventura
og Grøndahl Dreyer med i alt 10 opplag

Contents

Foreword

Never before has Mankind been in greater need of *user's manuals* than in our day.

In the past, Mankind has had to learn how to handle, use and store a stone, a knife, an axe, possibly a reaper, a horse, a person of the opposite sex and other simple objects. This could be handed down by word of mouth from parent to child.

This is no longer the case. Mankind is now surrounded by new, to some extent, very complicated objects (cassette tape recorders, electric shavers, wristwatches that tell the day and the week, charcoal grills, video players, typewriters with correcting keys, diesel engines, modern corkscrews, home computers, microwave ovens etc.), objects that are often totally unknown to Mankind's father and mother. Thus, the need for carefully-worked-out, instructive, preferably illustrated *user's manuals,* in our day, is palpable. And this need, of course, is increasing as constantly new aids and labour-saving, often idiotic, devices are forcing their way into Mankind's everyday life.

Another change that is taking place, and which has been taking place for some time, akin to what has been mentioned above, is the fact that Mankind no longer remains in his birthplace, not even in his own country, from the cradle to the grave. Mankind is now both here and there. More than ever before.

In short: *An internationalisation is taking place that is creating new demands for user's manuals.*

This internationalisation has resulted in the fact that the *Norwegian* is not always in Norway. He/she is to be found somewhere else, also during the off-season. And this tendency will increase when Norway gradually becomes a part of Europe, and the World, to a greater extent than ever before in history.

This, in turn, will result in thousands of *foreigners,* of various nationalities, in the days, the weeks and the years to come, encountering the Norwegian – professionally and/or socially – *for the first time.* And we are forced to assume that, to most foreigners, the Norwegian will be just as unknown, outlandish and incomprehensible an aid as the CD digital audio system, the combustion engine or «The Thinking Hotplate» were to our grandparents.

In other words, a new need has arisen for a manual about *How to understand and use a Norwegian in order to ensure the best possible results – as well as durability –* a guide to the correct treatment, balance, preservation, maintenance, adjustment and utilization of (as well as warnings against) the *Norwegian.**

---

* The *Norwegian* comes in a number of different models, sizes and sexes. Below, for practical reasons, these will all be designated as «The Norwegian».

Introduction

Congratulations on your acquisition of/encounter with a *Norwegian*.

We are certain that you will derive considerable pleasure from him/her in the future.

The *Norwegian* is a complicated, but robust and – with proper treatment – reliable object.

In order to ensure durability for him/her, and a warm friendship for yourself, we ask you to study this user's manual carefully before you start putting your new *Norwegian* to use.

With proper treatment, he/she will be able to provide you with a problem-free collaboration day after day and, in some cases, night after night, for many years to come.

Good luck!

Process of Manufacture

The Norwegian, in most cases, is manufactured in *Norway.* (See: *Norway (Place of Origin.)*)

The process itself is complicated and difficult to explain. In short, it involves an often problematic cooperation between the Norwegian's parents.

The manufacture is largely based on time-honoured, thoroughly tested methods that are rich in tradition, yet adapted to modern demands and prerequisites.

Most often, the manufacture takes place under a roof, but, as houses are few and far between in mountainous Norway, it is also done in the open air, for ex. in transit from place to place, in a boat, on skis etc. (See Fig. 1)

Previously, until a few years ago, it was customary for the Norwegian to be born *with skis on his feet.* But one of the improvements that has been made is that this is no longer the case.* Modern research has revealed, in fact, that this could be very uncomfortable and, to some extent, dangerous to the mother. For this reason, in our day, the Norwegian is not equipped with skis on his feet until sometime during the first year of life.

Another change/improvement, as far as skis are concerned, is the fact that the Norwegian is now able to take them off, as

---

* It still happens that the birth takes place with skis on the feet, but now it is most often the mother who has skis on during the birth.
** Among other things, this has resulted in considerable progress for the Norwegian National Football Team. The fact that Norway now goes and beats Italy, for example, is regarded by international football experts as a direct result of the fact that Norwegian football players no longer have to play with skis on their feet.

required, for. ex., in enclosed spaces such as planes, in smaller railway stations, in public toilets and similar places.**

Fig. 1. Examples of outdoor places of manufacture.

Norway (Place of Origin)

NORGE (Norway, Noruega, Norwegen) literally means, «The way to the North». Since the human race originated far to the south, in former times, there must have been a great many people who, at one time or another, headed northward – on «The way to the North». For various reasons, however, most of them stopped quite soon. Italians, Spaniards, Frenchmen, Greeks, etc., went no further north than to areas where they could make grapes grow and ripen. The Teutons, who were beer drinkers, didn't have to take this into consideration. So they headed further up in Northern Europe.

At that time Northern Europe was covered by a several thousand metre thick layer of ice and snow (The Ice Age – see Fig. 2). About 10,000 years ago, this ice started to melt and recede northward. Most of the Teutons were quite pleased with that. They were pretty fed up with ice and snow and everlasting winter fog. Many lay down in the grass and gazed at the drifting clouds and the first butterflies. Some wrote poems about the sun, while others started working on the trisection of the angle, and the like. They fell into pleasant habits, like raising grain and keeping livestock, which they ate instead of chasing about hunting for food, as they had done previously.

The Norwegian, on the other hand, who at that time, as has been mentioned, was born *with skis on his feet,* felt helpless and clumsy among the grass and flowers (see: *Norwegian Self-Consciousness*). He wanted skiing conditions. He wanted snow. And so he took along his women and children, and followed the glacier on its wanderings northward. When he came to what was later called «Norway», he discovered that he

Fig. 2 The Ice Age (detail). The Sorbonne in Paris (cross-section) inset to show dimensions.

could go no further, and so he settled down there.

But the ice continued to melt, so that sometimes, during the summer, skiing conditions are also poor in Norway. And in our day, now that the Norwegian, as has been mentioned before, can take off his skis when necessary, it happens that he begins to suspect that people from more southerly and, therefore, warmer parts of the globe have found better places in which to live. *But he conceals this suspicion, especially from his children.**

Norway was formerly quite a wild and disorderly land. Among other things, Norway was famous as a place where polar bears prowled about the streets. This is no longer the case. Now, when one or two polar bears may periodically be seen in the streets, this is more often due to a misunderstanding than genuine polar bears. If, in our day, you should see a polar bear in a Norwegian street, especially in the dead of night, you should tentatively say to the animal: «Good evening?» If the polar bear answers, «Shutyourbigmouth!» or something that sounds like this, in all likelihood, this is not a

---

* For this reason, in order to give his children something different to think about, he teaches them quite early that people who live further south than Norway are: 1) unreliable, 2) lazy, 3) depraved, 4) Catholic and 5) stupid, have a poor education and tend to be racially prejudiced. In addition, they reek of garlic and, at all times, are under the influence of alcohol and / or narcotics.

Since every known people, apart from a few nomadic Eskimos, live further south than Norway, the above-mentioned characteristics apply to quite a large number of the earth's inhabitants.

polar bear but a Norwegian on his way home from a party. (See Fig. 3) (See also: *The Norwegian and Intoxication*)

Fig. 3 A misunderstanding, or a Norwegian on his way home from a party.

The Norwegian

A *Eyes*
Have a tendency to look askance at Sweden, Europe and USA, as well as a tendency to look back on the time the World was young, Norwegian skiers won the most during the Winter Olympics and corrupt politicians and unreliable officials were something that occurred in Denmark, Germany, England, Spain, Naples and the rest of Italy, Egypt and the rest of Africa, USA, South and Central America and *most other places south of Svinesund.*

B *National Pride*
Is located on top of the head, under the hair, and for this and other reasons may be difficult to detect. (See: *Norwegian National Pride – Fact and Fantasy*)

C *Mouth*
Is used for the intake of food

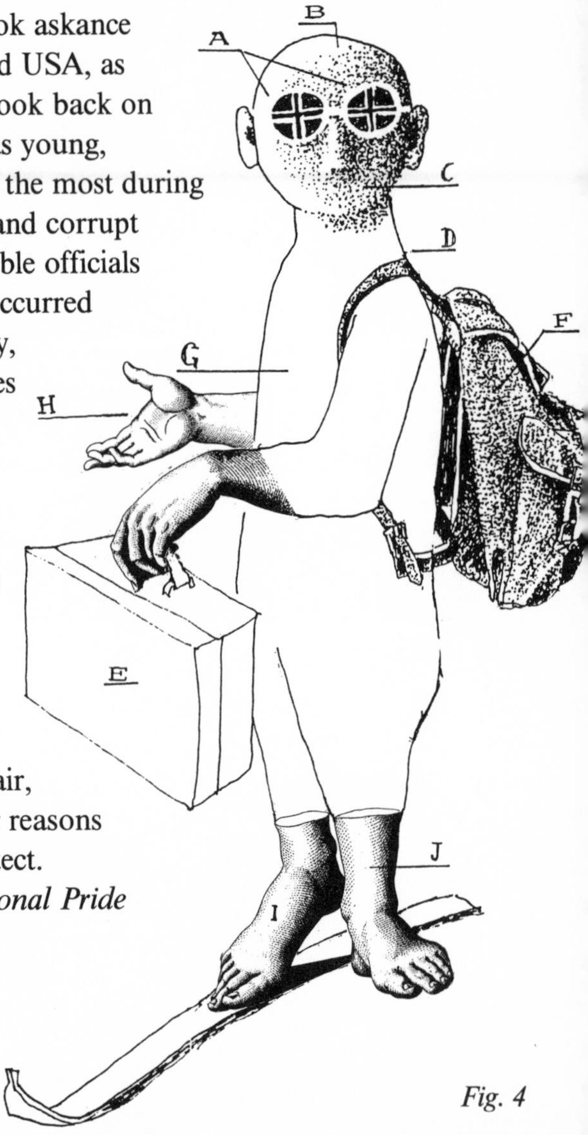

Fig. 4

and drink (See: *Norwegian Eating Habits and The Norwegian and Intoxication*), and, to some extent, for talking. (See: *Norwegian Conversations (Do they Occur?)*)

D *Centre of Self-Consciousness*
Is to be found between the shoulderblades and is a prime mover in the Norwegian. (See: *Norwegian Self-Consciousness*)

E *Suitcase*
Contains more recent European and other foreign influence.

F *Rucksack*
For carrying the Norwegian cultural heritage. This was previously quite full of folktales, legends, attitudes towards life, belief, disbelief, etc., but is now relatively deflated. (See: *The Heritage of the Fathers*)

G *Craving for Freedom*
Located in the heart. (See: *Craving for Freedom*)

H *Right Hand*
Open, ready to accept friendship and/or sales contracts.

I *Right Foot*
Anchored in Norwegian tradition and history.

J *Left Foot*
Taking the first, tentative steps into Europe and the rest of the World.

Distinguishing marks

How can one tell if the Norwegian is a Norwegian, and not something entirely different?

If one finds oneself in Norway, and masters the Norwegian language, this is relatively easy. One may apply the Law of Probability: Most people who live and stay in Norway, and who speak Norwegian, are Norwegians.

But how can one recognize a Norwegian if one encounters him outside of Norway? In London? In Paris? In Tokyo? The Norwegian has a number of racial characteristics: fair skin, mousy hair, big hands and feet, etc. But these characteristics are also to be found among other Germanic people. Thus, in our day, it may be difficult to tell a Norwegian from, for example, a Swede, a German, an Austrian or a Dutchman. Formerly, in the old days, the Norwegian was easily recognizable: No matter where in the world he found himself, he wore a knitted woolen cap with a pompom on his head. In addition, he gave off a faint odour of fish, his name was Ola or Kari* and he said very little. And if he did say something, he said that: Everybody who lived south of the Skagerrak was a pickpocket by nature and profession, that he didn't trust Jews, Catholics, Gypsies and almost everybody else, and that

* This is no longer the case. Because the Norwegian's parents wanted to
  find a name for him that wasn't usual at the time he was to be
  christened, the Norwegian, today, may be named: Arnhold, Ausgard,
  Argot, Altur, Agerd, Borgur, Bolle, Bro, Gro, Gru, Gruhild, Grom.
  Grams, Gry, Grytte, Harry, Hurry, Hanker, Hester, Hunker, Heltora,
  Haltora, Hastur, Hultin, etc.
    In other words: The Norwegian today may be named anything at all
  – except Adolf, Adolph, Vidkun, Vidgun, Joseph, Heinrich, Buddha,
  Judas or Xpezguard.

Fig. 5 Businessmen from many lands, in a body, in St. Peter's Square in Rome.

Norwegian meatballs, skiers, dentists, boat constructors, seamen, etc., were the best in the world.*

In short: Formerly, at the time the Norwegian was named Ola or Kari, the Norwegian was a kind of wild, cantankerous ape from the mountains and the fjords, and, therefore, easily recognizable among the people of the earth no matter where he found himself.

But now? In the 1990's?

Now, that he may be named almost anything at all, is dressed in clothes that are made in Italy, shoes that are made in Portugal, eats with a knife and a fork, often appears without skis on his feet and sometimes has brown eyes? How can you tell if the Norwegian is a Norwegian now, if you meet him among many other people? For example: among businessmen from many lands, in a body, in St. Peter's Square in Rome? (See Fig. 5). How will you be able to tell him apart from the rest?

You can ask him, of course: «Are you Norwegian?»

But it's not certain that he understands the question. It depends on which language you are speaking when you ask him.

The best way to tell whether the Norwegian is a Norwegian is to say: «Are you Swedish?»

Regardless of whether you say this in English, French, Italian, Japanese, Urdu or Swahili, he will answer:

«Swedish? Me? I'm a Norwegian!»

Then you will be able to tell.

* He may still believe this, but he no longer says it out loud.

Norwegian Conversations (Do they Occur?)

Except under special circumstances, the Norwegian, by nature and tradition, is a silent person. For this reason, Silence in Norway is connected with Wisdom.

In Norwegian culture there are several proverbs that express this view: «Speech is silver, but silence is golden.» «Still waters run deep.» «Empty barrels make the most noise.» To name a few.

Like most national characteristics, The Norwegian Silence and The Norwegian Distrust of Conversations and Small Talk have a historical-geographical-climatical explanation:

For 8000 years, every single Norwegian lived in his very own cave (See: *Norwegian Self-Consciousness*), by his very own fjord or on his very own mountain, surrounded only by his closest family. In other words: *For 8000 years the Norwegian had no one to talk with* apart from members of his closest family – and what does one talk with them about, when one has been with them day and night for 8000 years? Indeed!

For this reason, the Norwegian was completely silent for 8000 years.

In the course of this time, naturally, he was not without a certain need to communicate. When this need became too great, he went outside, found a flat stone and carved a message on it.

Carving letters – Runes – on stone was quite hard and time-consuming work with the tools of the day. For this reason, the messages were comparatively short: «I, Halgrim, carved this stone» or «I, Halgrim» or simply «I».

Or something similar.

After 8000 years, the Norwegian saw other people (neighbours) for the first time, but from a very great distance – on the other mountain, or on the other side of the fjord. So he began to communicate with them, but, because of the distance, this also had to be rather brief: «Go away!»

He didn't shout, «I love you!» for example, because self-conscious people (See: *Norwegian Self-Consciousness*) don't shout that sort of thing. At that time, however, the Norwegian had other opportunities of expressing himself. He could

Fig. 6 Example of a Norwegian conversation.

express irritation or anger by going outside and chopping down a tree, or throwing big stones in the water.* And if he wanted to express love, he could go into the forest, kill an elk or a bear, put the animal on his back and carry it with him and drop it in the lap of his beloved. That meant: «I love you. I shall safeguard and protect you, and provide you and our children with fresh meat in good days and bad, until death do us part – and, if possible, without Norway becoming a member of EC.»

In our time, the Norwegian does not have the same opportunity of expressing himself as he did then. One has to own a forest in order to be able to chop down trees, the bear is unconditionally preserved and elk may only be shot during the hunting season, in the autumn. Whereas love may arise at any time of the year. A few, now living Norwegians express themselves by going on skis across Greenland, or by sailing across the Atlantic Ocean in a wicker basket, but most of them no longer have the time nor the opportunity for that sort of thing.

At any rate: An 8000-year-old habit of carving messages on stones with a blunt tool, or screeching through the wind at great distances, has not resulted in any great ability or desire to carry on long conversations.

In addition, it is cold in Norway. At twenty degrees below zero, centigrade, one does not remain seated at a sidewalk cafe for any length of time in order to converse about art, food, cheese, football, the year's wine harvest, love or The Meaning of Life.

When the Norwegian wishes to express his opinion about one of these or similar topics, he does it at home. *He doesn't talk about it, but writes a book about it, or writes a letter about it and sends this letter to his local newspaper.*

Norway is the one country in the World that has the most writers and the most local newspapers in relation to the population.

* As is known, the Norwegian coast is surrounded by thousands of larger and smaller stones (The Skerries). This is very likely a sign that there was considerable irritation during the Norwegian Stone Age.

The Norwegian and Intoxication

Because (See: *Norwegian Self-Consciousness* and *Norwegian Conversations (Do They Occur?)*) the Norwegian lived alone in his cave for 8000 years, there was no commercial basis for the manufacture of alcohol in Norway at that time. Thus, the Norwegian had to fend for himself in this area. He produced his own alcoholic beverages at home in the cave, later on the farm. However, he had not learned how to produce glass and bottles, and so the storage of the finished product became a problem for him.

He solved this problem by drinking everything up at once.

Afterwards, when he went out into the forest, he was cheerful and happy, and kindly disposed towards the whole world. Thus, on a day like this, if he met an elk, a bear or something similar, he often went over to the elk or the bear, or whatever it was, and said, for ex., «You're a decent sort.» And showed signs of wanting to pat the animal on its head. The animal, which was quite sober, regarded this friendliness as a threat (sober animals and people in Norway, and other places, often do), and, in some instances, killed the Norwegian, or bit off one or more arms and legs.

These experiences, as well as the hereditary lack of empty bottles, have resulted in the Norwegian's 1) having considerable respect for intoxication, which he knows may lead to misunderstandings and unpleasantness in the forest, and, therefore, 2) drinking everything up today, because he doesn't know whether he will be alive in the morning.

From a statistical point of view, the Norwegian's consumption of alcohol is very low as compared with that of others:

In one year, the Dane drinks, statistically, 11 litres of wine, 116 litres of beer and 1,7 litres of distilled alcohol.

The corresponding figures for the Frenchman are: 101, 45,2 and 3,5; for the Englishman: 5,7, 118 and 4,1; for the German: 22, 148 and 4,1.

While the Norwegian drinks only 3,2 litres of wine, 45,1 litres of beer and 1,2 litres of distilled alcohol. Statistically. Annually.

In spite of the fact that the Norwegian's consumption of alcohol is one of the lowest in Europe, it may sometimes seem and, not least, sound as if this is not the case. This is due to the fact that, while the Dane, the Englishman, the Frenchman etc. drink a little every day, throughout the entire statistical period, the Norwegian, for the above-mentioned reasons, often drinks up the entire statistics all at once. Often on the boat to Denmark, or on other trips abroad. And then it may often *seem* as if 3.2 litres of wine, 45,1 litres of beer and 1,2 litres of distilled alcohol are more than they really are. Statistically.

Just as the intoxicated Norwegian, in the past, went out into the forest and talked in a friendly manner to bears and elks, so the Norwegian today will do something similar. Whether he finds himself on the boat to Denmark, or in a city somewhere else in the World, after drinking up the annual statistics he is cheerful, happy and kindly disposed. Sometimes he will go out onto the dance floor, or into the street, and say to people he meets: «Hello there! Hello there!» And make signs that he would like to pat them on the head, or on other places. Many foreigners, like elks and bears in the past, misunderstand this and regard the Norwegian as a threat, and snub him. This

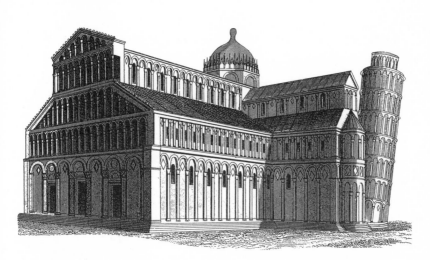

Fig. 7 Possible consequences of Norwegian intoxication and/or self-consciousness.

makes the Norwegian sad, and he may (See: *Norwegian Self-Consciousness*) start flailing his arms and, out of pure helplessness, behave unfortunately and knock down waiters and other things. (See Fig. 7)

In an intoxicated state the Norwegian, sometimes becomes talkative. He then commands several foreign languages (English, French, Italian, Russian, etc.) which he otherwise does not know. And during the evening he solves most of the World's problems.

If the American and/or the Russian president, and others with power and influence over the future of the World, had listened to, taken notice of and learned from an intoxicated Norwegian, the World could have been quite different from the way she is today.

Norwegian Self-Consciousness

The basis for the Norwegian Self-Consciousness is somewhat vague, and, like most phenomena, probably has several causes.

One of the causes, of course, is this business of the skis. (See: *Norway (Place of Origin)*).

Another reason is undoubtedly the fact that for 8000 years the Norwegian lived more or less alone – first in a cave, later in a house, on a mountain, an island or at the head of a fjord – surrounded only by his closest familiy. Then, when he met other people for the first time, about 2000 years ago for ex., while on a sailing trip abroad, he felt helpless. He didn't know what to say to them. He felt that he had enormous feet, each with the big toe on the right side, etc.

During the first 400–500 years of this period («The Viking Age»), this helplessness often resulted in his hitting out in all directions with sharp objects (swords, spears), throwing stones, tearing down nunneries and church steeples, and doing other awkward and unfortunate things *because he didn't otherwise know what to do in order to establish contact with other people.*

During this period, the Norwegian was often misunderstood by foreigners – and this is still the case. Because, even in our day, owing to hereditary self-consciousness and feelings of helplessness, it happens that the Norwegian can tear down smaller church steeples, etc., when in reality he means something entirely different.

A third reason for The Norwegian Self-Consciousness is that, even though the Norwegian often lives in cities and suburban areas, he always knows that *he is one of few,* i.e.

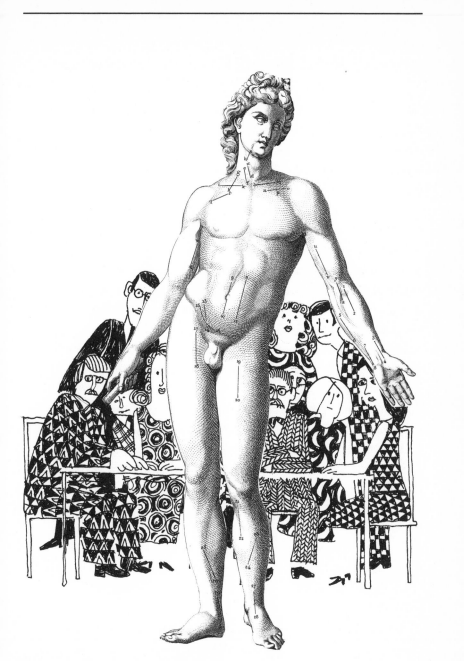

Fig. 8 A feeling of being observed.

one of 4,5 million. (An Indian, for ex., knows that he is one of 800 million, i.e. one of many). This knowledge has always made the Norwegian feel that he was more or less in a class by himself, and, therefore, important and interesting. And worthy of note. For this reason, it is easy for him to believe that he is being observed, *that people are looking at him.* (See Fig. 8)

Thus, when he has to go through a restaurant, or another large room where there are a lot of strangers, he assumes that all of these strangers are looking at him as he walks there. And naturally, his body and limbs stiffen, and he may easily overturn glasses, tables, headwaiters, etc., *and this doesn't make things easier for him.*

It is on such occasions that the Norwegian feels that he has unusually big feet. And big hands. Hands like bunches of bananas. Bunches of bananas like the ones that have been hanging in the shop too long. He doesn't know where to put these hands, *if he doesn't have big pockets to put them in.*

The Norwegian likes clothes with big pockets.

It is possible that, if the Vikings had had clothes with big pockets, The Viking Age would have turned out differently.

The Heritage of the Fathers

Until a few years ago, the Norwegian carried most of his philosophies, opinions, attitudes and convictions on his back, one might say. These opinions, attitudes and convictions had been handed down to him by his parents, and, in turn, had been handed down to them by *their* parents, backwards.

Among these handed down opinions, attitudes and convictions were:

1) Speech is silver but silence is golden.

2) Norway is the most beautiful and the best country in Scandinavia, and Scandinavia, without comparison, is the most beautiful part of the world.

3) Norwegian doctors are the only doctors in the world who have a proper medical training. Among other things, they are the only doctors who have learned anything about hygiene.

4) Norwegian politicians, functionaries, policemen, waiters and taxi drivers are honest as opposed to foreign (also Swedish) politicans, functionaries, policemen, waiters and taxi drivers, who are corrupt, untruthful, greedy for power and unreliable.

5) Norwegian skiers are the best in the world, and if foreign (for ex. Swedish) skiers ski faster than Norwegians, this is because they have either taken anabolic steroids and/or have been paid by the Government, or the Norwegians have used the wrong ski wax or eaten something that disagreed with them.

6) In Norway, only thieves steal, while everybody steals abroad, unless you watch your suitcase closely.

7) Henrik Ibsen is the greatest dramatist in the World.

8) Norwegian food is really the only food fit for human consumption.

9) All Norwegians are individualists.

10) There is reason to view with suspicion: electronic data processing, TV surveillance, outboard motors, etc.

11) Being rich won't make you happy.

12) One should drink water with one's food.

13) One should view with suspicion: Italians, Frenchmen, Dutchmen, Swedes, Spaniards, Greeks *and most other foreigners over or under 18 years of age.*

The modern Norwegian has discarded, and disposed of, much of The Heritage of His Fathers. This is true of points 4, 6, 10, 11 and 12.

The Norwegian's Craving for Freedom

Deep in his heart, the Norwegian has a great craving for freedom. He reacts quickly and violently to anything that might seem like a curtailment of his freedom and independence and sense of justice. Like so many other things, the origins and explanation of this have been conditioned by history, geography and climate.

When Norway was united into a single kingdom (King Harald Fairhair around the year 870), every single Norwegian had been living for 9000 years as his own king, by his fjord, or on his mountain, or in his valley. The unification of Norway into a single kingdom, in all likelihood, didn't make much of an impression on the Norwegian at the time it took place. He found that having a king was quite all right, as long as the fellow had sense enough to remain at home and not think he was someone special.

In addition, in a number of valleys and outlying districts, there were many people who weren't even aware of the fact that the land *had been* united into a single kingdom until the EC Referendum in 1972.

In any case: this nearly 9000-year-old habit of deciding everything oneself, without any meddling except, possibly, from one's closest family, became lodged, and is still lodged, in the present Norwegian's heart. He has a clear tendency to react negatively to every law and regulation that is issued by anyone other than his wife.

On this point, the Norwegian differs enormously from the Swede.

Many foreigners get all mixed up, when they try to tell the difference between the Norwegian and the Swede. They readily believe that Stockholm is an island off the western coast of Norway, or that Bjørn Borg is a town by the Oslo Fjord, and may believe that the difference between the Norwegian and the Swede boils down to a slight difference in dialects.

This is not the case.

As far as the craving for freedom is concerned, the difference between the Norwegian and the Swede is enormous.

When, for ex., the regulation about wearing seat belts came into effect in Sweden, the Swede wore the seat belt at every opportunity. In many instances, the Swede wears a seat belt even when he isn't going to drive a car. Many Swedes *who don't own a car, and who have never ever thought about buying a car,* buy a seat belt in order to enable themselves to follow the regulation about wearing seat belts.

On the other hand, when the regulation about wearing seat belts came into effect in Norway, this resulted in a storm of protests from Norwegian organizations and individuals. Hundreds of indignant letters to the editor were written and printed in Norwegian newspapers. The Norwegian regarded such a regulation as an encroachment of Human Rights, and a glaring example of a breach of man's inherent right to control his own life and his own future and, in addition, as a threat to Freedom of Choice, Freedom of the Press, etc.

However, the regulation didn't prevent the Norwegian from wearing the seat belt. At the time the regulation came into effect, the Norwegian had been wearing the seat belt, on every occasion, for many years, and didn't want such an idiotic regulation to cause him to break such an excellent habit.

Thus, as far as regulations about seat belts are concerned,

like so many other things, it may appear to a foreigner that the Norwegian and the Swede react more or less in the same way. *Both wear seat belts.* And he may, therefore, believe that the two are more or less alike. But, as has been explained above, this is not the case: The Swede obeys every old and new regulation – period. The Norwegian also obeys every regulation, but protests against it in the newspapers.

The Norwegian's craving for freedom is so great that, every now and then, when he believes that the regulations have become too many and too severe, he gives a good deal of thought to doing something about it.

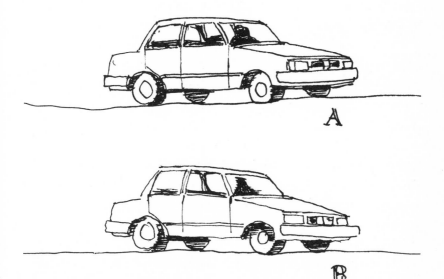

Fig. 9 Example of different kinds of craving for freedom:
A. Swedish bread-winner on his way home from work.
B. Norwegian bread-winner on his way home from work.

Up to now he hasn't done anything.

There may be several explanations of this apparent passivity:

1. There was a European Cup Football Match on TV that evening.

2. It was raining, or

3. The weather was exceptionally good, with sunshine, so he took a walk, or went to his cabin instead.

Or something similar.

The Norwegian and Mysticism

Fig. 10

The Norwegian is a sober person. His relationship to God is somewhat like his relationship to the King. He believes that God (and the King) is quite all right – on the condition that He behaves like a proper Norwegian and doesn't believe that He is anything special. The Norwegian doesn't say this outright, but he believes that God (and the King), in spite of everything, is no more than human.

The Norwegian wouldn't be surprised if, one day, he should see God (or the King) ahead of him in a bus queue, for ex., or on Karl Johansgate in Oslo. (See Fig. 10).

Norwegian National Pride – Fact and Fantasy

The Norwegian is very proud of his country, his country's nature, with mountains and fjords, of his country's system of government, and of all his fellow countrymen who have made names for themselves abroad.*

In other words, the Norwegian has an intense feeling of national pride. But because this is located on top of his head, under the hair, it is not very easy to detect.

Nor is it any easier to detect when the Norwegian, at every opportunity, makes disparaging remarks about the country, the people, the Norwegian mountains, the climate, Norwegian newspapers, the television programs, the Norwegian education system, the health and social services and the incumbent Prime Minister.

He says, willingly and often, for ex., that Norwegian politicians, Norwegian car repair shops, Norwegian waiters, Norwegian parking metre attendants, Norwegian summers and Norwegian ski jumpers are the worst, most expensive, slowest, most insolent, wettest and poorest in the whole World.

Foreigners may misunderstand this.

Foreigners may believe, and often do, that when the Norwegian says that Norwegian politicians, car repair shops, waiters, parking metre attendants, summers and ski jumpers are the worst, most expensive, slowest, most insolent, wettest and poorest in the World, this is because he doesn't like Norwegian politicians, car repair shops, waiters, parking metre attendants, summers and ski jumpers. The fact is, however, that regardless of what he says, the Norwegian *believes* that

* There is a long list of world famous Norwegians that only Norwegians have heard of.

Norwegian politicians, Norwegian car repair shops, Norwegian waiters, Norwegian parking metre attendants, Norwegian summers and Norwegian ski jumpers are the most honest, cleverest, quickest, politest, most beautiful and best in the World – and, in addition, the only ones who can execute a perfect Telemark Turn.

WARNING

When the Norwegian says that Norwegian politicians, doctors, parking metre attendants, etc., are the worst, poorest, laziest, etc., in the world, you must not agree out of politeness. I mean: Of course you may say whatever you like, but, if you still wish to derive happiness from your Norwegian, say something else.

Otherwise, the Norwegian is famous for being outspoken. Thus, he may be a poor diplomat, because he places honesty above, for ex., Politeness and Considerateness.

Because the Norwegian is famous for his tactlessness, there is a general misunderstanding among foreigners that he tells the truth. That he says, at all times, exactly what he means. *As a rule* he does tell the plain, often unvarnished, truth – but *there are always exceptions.* One, as has been mentioned above, is when he talks about Norway and Norwegian conditions. There is one other exception:

When/if the Norwegian has been elected to a responsible position, such as Prime Minister, director of the choir, boss of the factory, chairman of the board of the housing cooperative, etc., he *thinks: «I've deserved this. This is going to be fun. I'll do very well, because, obviously, I'm one who is best qualified for the job. Now they're going to see that I will lead the country, the choir, the factory or the housing cooperative to greater heights, and make it the best in Europe.»*

This, as a rule, is what he *thinks.*

But what he *says* in his speech, during the dinner afterwards, is as follows:

«When I agreed to take on this great and difficult position, I did so, not because I believe I am the right man for this challenging task that lies ahead of us – I am the first to admit that I am a very ordinary person, totally lacking in the qualities and dimensions of my predecessor. There are many of you here today who are far better qualified for this position of leadership than I am. Perhaps every one of you.

I do not go to this task with a light heart, but as long as the party, the choir, the factory or the housing cooperative has now asked me to take this on, and has use for me, I feel it is my duty to say yes.

I hope you will all help me in the future. I am counting on you, and you can count on me, to the extent of my modest abilities, to do the best I can. Thank you.»

WARNING

See the previous WARNING. The same
applies here, no less.

Norwegian Eating Habits

The Norwegian is used to eating few, but substantial, meals.
The European habit of eating a long lunch in the middle of
the workday is unknown to him. This is because he has, and
always did have, a relatively long way to go between his
domicile and his place of work. During The Viking Age he
lived, of course, in Norway, but went to work on Greenland,
Iceland, The Isle of Man, Normandie, etc. Thus, it was out of
the question for him to come home for lunch between twelve
and two o'clock. Later, his work again took him a long way
from home: in the deep forests, on another mountain or at
sea, catching fish. For this reason, he was accustomed to
eating well before setting out, for ex., for Greenland in the
morning, and waiting to eat his next meal until he came back
in the evening – possibly at Christmas.

By and large, the modern Norwegian likes all kinds of food.
    Among the Norwegian specialities that have been handed
down from ancient times we would like to mention *lutefisk*.
Lutefisk is fish steeped in *lut* (or lye) until it has a consistency,
smell and taste in a class by itself. It is very difficult to describe
the way *lutefisk* looks. The closest we can come is to compare
it with a certain type of slimy monster that sometimes appears
in American and Japanese horror films (See Fig. 11).
    Foreigners are advised not to eat *lutefisk*, because no one
likes *lutefisk* unless one has eaten it, more or less regularly, for
about 90 years. For the same reason, there are very few
Norwegians who like *lutefisk*. Even so, the reason why *lutefisk*
is sold and eaten in such great quantities in Norway may have
something to do with national obstinacy and the fact that it is

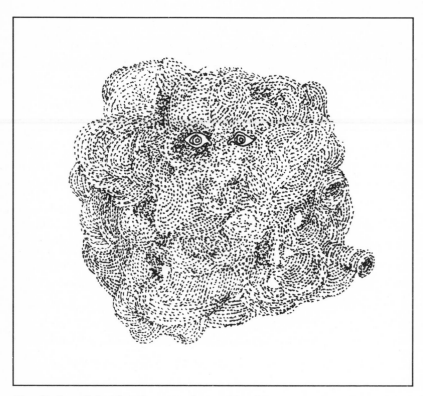

Fig. 11 Lutefisk *(detail, somewhat reduced).*

regarded as having a certain pedagogical value: Children are supposed to learn to suffer in silence, and accustom themselves to The Vicissitudes of Life: If you can manage to swallow *lutefisk*, you can also manage to swallow The Disappointments of Life (unhappy love affairs, broken dreams, annulled sales contracts, etc.).

In addition to *lutefisk*, the Norwegian eats many other kinds of fish. He has always eaten a lot of fish, which is not surprising since we know that the Norwegian has always lived – and, in most cases, still lives – in the vicinity of water.

For this reason, it is very natural that the Norwegian is a very eager fisherman, despite the fact that this is no longer his profession. Even now, when he can (and does) buy boneless, rectangular fish from the frozen fish counter, the Norwegian loves to go fishing in his spare time.

Even Norwegians who don't really like fish are eager fishermen. They catch fish because, as children, they were forced to eat up all the fish (and bones), which they had for dinner five days a week. They go fishing *and clobber the fish to death in order to avenge themselves.*

Formerly, while the Norwegian was still living in Norway – before he had become a «European» – he usually drank water or milk with his meals. Now he would rather drink wine, but prefers wine with a taste he is more or less accustomed to: namely, wine that tastes like water, milk or fried mackerel.

The Norwegian and the Wilderness

By tradition, nature and upbringing, the Norwegian is a hunter, a fisherman and a whaler (with skis on his feet). But, in practice, the contemporary Norwegian lives, more or less, like other people in the civilized world. He lives in a house with windows, doors, a roof and central heating. He has a TV, telephone, electric shaver, shoes, socks, wristwatch, a knife and a fork and he eats food that is often boiled or fried.

In other words: He has almost everything. *But he doesn't like it.*

The Norwegian's ideal is to be a son/daughter of the Sea, the Mountain, the Rustling Forest – in short, a son/daughter of the Wilderness, independent of the namby-pamby, European lowlands civilization, with all its unnecessary luxury and comfort. A silent, pensive and unfettered bird who flies his own way. This is the Norwegian's ideal – and so he buys a *hytte*, if he can afford one.

A *hytte* is a tiny, little house in the Wilderness.

The ideal location for a *hytte* is up on a mountaintop, or on a skerry all the way out by the sea, far from any neighbours. But even in Norway, which abounds in mountaintops and skerries, it has become more and more difficult to find a lonely mountaintop that has not already been discovered by someone else. And so the Norwegian often has to share his lonely mountaintop, or his lonely skerry, with other free, unfettered birds. However, he builds a high fence between himself and his neighbours, and pretends they don't exist. At any rate, he doesn't speak to them, and even though they have been his neighbours all his life he doesn't even know their names.

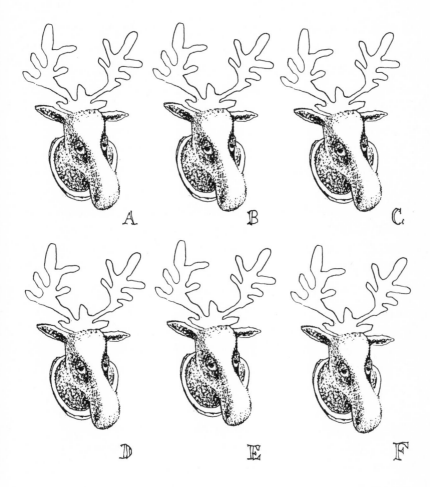

Fig. 12 Tools and apparatus in use at the hytte. *A: Telephone B: Telefax C: TV apparatus D: Electric Iron E: Can opener F: Power saw.*

The Norwegian loves his *hytte* and is there whenever the demands of the modern age permit: during summer holidays, at Christmas, Easter, etc. In addition to being very tiny, the *hytte* is very sparsely furnished, with an open fire and an earthen floor. He has to fetch water from a well that is 250 metres away. In general, the *hytte* is totally different from the civilized, European dwelling in which he is forced to live throughout the rest of the year. It is a den that is suited to a son/daughter of the Wilderness, and, while they are young, to his/her children.

However, it happens, in most instances, that the Norwegian's children grow bigger, and then they often hate the *hytte* because it's so boring there. Because there are no kiosks or video shops, or because no rock concerts are arranged in the vicinity and because there is no one of the same age to talk with (there are probably children of the same age on the other side of the fence, but even children know that they're not supposed to have anything to do with *them*).

In order to keep peace in the family, the Norwegian has therefore laid planks on the earthen floor, built on one or two children's rooms and a TV room and added a number of other modern conveniences. But because the Norwegian is, after all, a son/daughter of the Wilderness, who lives a simple life in harmony with Nature, he has concealed the telephone in a rustic bookcase (behind the Bible and a Handbook on Trout Fishing), hidden the telefax in a rose-painted wooden chest with iron bands, and covered the electric oven with pebbles. The electric shaver is camouflaged as a can of ski wax for crusted snow. (See Fig. 12).

Why the Norwegian feels this deep, uncivilized urge to be a child of Nature is still a mystery to Science.

It may be due to the fact that his forefathers were simple farmers and fishermen, who lived in harmony with nature. But the same may also be said about the forefathers of most people. Even the forefathers of the Parisians were probably farmers and fishermen (French), without this apparently making contemporary Parisians feel the need to live on mountaintops, eat raw eggs or speak in sentences of one syllable.

There has to be an explanation and as has been said: Science is working on it.

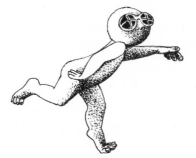

The Norwegian and the Foreigner

As has been mentioned above:

The Norwegian is a sober person.

He knows that he lives, and has always lived, on the fringe of the World. On the outermost fringe of Europe. Thus, he has a tendency, especially in certain areas of breeding, to assume that people who live in the centre are better at choosing the correct attire when going to the opera, to a restaurant or to a fashion show, and more confident about using the correct knife for different kinds of food, etc.

In short: On various occasions, when the Norwegian is with foreigners, he may feel like a babe in the foreign woods. Far from Mother and Dad and his Grandparents. In addition, he sometimes has the feeling that these foreigners want to cheat him, take his lunch packet, give him the wrong change, or steal his Fisheries Agreement, etc.

But, because he is a proud son/daughter of the Wilderness (See: *The Norwegian and the Wilderness*), he will not admit these childish feelings to himself or to anyone else. And so he tries to conceal them in various ways: like calling the waiter names, arguing with the taxi driver, knocking down smaller church steeples (See: *Norwegian Self-Consciousness*), staring at the wall instead of signing the contract, or disturbing the peace in the street or in the Metro.

The most sensible thing the foreigner can do, when he encounters the Norwegian in this state of mind, is to pretend that nothing has happened, and/or talk about something different, such as, for ex., the weather, The World's Fair in Paris in 1900, The Decline and Fall of the Roman Empire, or about anything at all.

Fig. 13 A Norwegian among foreigners.

The Norwegian Language

When the Norwegian speaks with other Norwegians, he speaks *Norwegian*, an ancient language in the Germanic Family of Languages, which resembles most other languages insofar as Coca Cola in Norwegian is «Coca Cola». And in the same way:

Camping = camping
Snack bar = snack bar
Discotheque = discoteque
Fast food = fast food
Junk food = junk food
Instant coffee = instant coffee
Supermarket = supermarked
Donald Duck = Donald Duck
USA = USA
etc.

In the Norwegian language, however, there are certain *words* that are not to be found in other languages: «Bikkje», «Riksmeglingsmann», «Fylkesreguleringsarkitekt», «Vinmonopolbestyrer», «Bevegelighelligdag», «Dagfør-elleretterbevegelighelligdag», etc. *)

In addition, there is a wide selection of words in the Norwegian language that stands for things, acts and conditions typical of, and of considerable significance and interest to, the Norwegian people and their way of life and

*) Dog (slang), State Mediator, Chief county planning architect, Manager of the State Wine and Liquor Monopoly, Flexible holiday, Day before or after a flexible holiday, etc.)

culture. There is, for ex., an exceptional number of names for various kinds of fish (raw or processed), winds, cold, frostbite, tax burdens, levies, alcoholic beverages and the consequences of their use, skiing conditions and rainy weather and quite a lot of (about 70) different names for disagreeable and undesirable neighbours and their children.

Where to use a Norwegian

Fig. 14

You may use a Norwegian as a friend, a football player, a business or sexual partner, enemy, cook, errand boy on a bike, fisherman, farmer, director, eye specialist, etc. In short: You may use the Norwegian for most of the things a human being may be used for, with the exception of certain duties that are prohibited by your country (King, Prime Minister, Tribal Chieftain, etc.), as well as, except in emergencies, a Catholic priest, nun, Indian fakir, etc.

How to Use a Norwegian

When you want the Norwegian to carry out your instructions, just ask him in a friendly and civil manner to comply with your request. If this doesn't produce satisfactory results, there is a defect. In such cases, use *The Trouble-Shooter's Guide*.

Trouble-Shooter's Guide

Defect	Possible Cause	Remedy
You ask the Norwegian to go to the left, but he goes to the right.	He has had an attack of homesickness, and is lost in thought. Perhaps he is reminiscing about his childhood summers with his Grandmother and Grandfather and is unable to hear what you are saying because, in his inner ear, he can hear his grandfather's clock ticking on the parlour wall.	Give him a cup of coffee and try again.
You ask the Norwegian to go to the left, but he goes to the right.	He hasn't understood your question.	Ask him again in a different way. (Sign language, a diagram, etc.)
You ask the Norwegian to go to the left, but he goes neither to the left nor to the right. He turns on his heel and goes back to the hotel.	He has had an attack of «Craving for Freedom» (See: *The Norwegian's Craving for Freedom*), and won't let a foreigner tell him where to go.	Ask him to go back to the hotel, and he will *not* go back to the hotel.

Defect	Possible Cause	Remedy
You ask the Norwegian to go to the right, but he doesn't go to the right. He sits down on the curbstone.	Because of his suspicion of long conversations (See: *Norwegian Conversations (Do They Occur)*), he thinks there's too much talk and too little action.	Go down on one knee, as if for the start of the 100-metre sprint. Start running in the desired direction. Then he will follow in order to take part in the competition.
You ask the Norwegian to sign, for ex., a Fisheries Agreement. He doesn't sign, but remains seated and stares at the wall.	He thinks you are trying to swindle him and remembers the time his great-great-great-grandfather was swindled out of a load of timber in Enkhuisen, Holland in 1863. 2. He is right: You are trying to swindle him.	Tell him that everybody, even your great-great-great-grandfather was swindled in Enkhuisen, Holland in 1863. 2. Stop it: Write a new contract and ask him to sign it.
You ask the Norwegian to sign, for ex., a Fisheries Agreement. He doesn't sign it, but throws the fountain pen out through the closed window, at the same time as he overturns the water carafe standing on the table.	He suddenly, and self-consciously, feels that he is being observed by the rest of the group around the table (See: *Norwegian Self-Consciousness*), and doesn't know what to do or where to put his hands.	Behave as if nothing has happened. Give him a new fountain pen, while talking about something different, for ex., Italian football or the weather.

Defect	Possible Cause	Remedy
You take the Norwegian with you in order to show him something that you are proud of in your home town (St. Peter's, the Pyramid of Cheops, The Nelson Column, the Eiffel Tower, The Prado Museum, the Bajrakli Mosque, etc.) and expect him to clap his hands for joy, while uttering cries of delight. He doesn't do it. He just stands there, and doesn't even take a picture of the object.	Because of National Pride he stands there and says to himself, «Well, well, it *is* nice, but think of the cost in human toil and poverty and oppression. And besides it's nothing compared with the Holmenkollen Ski Jump or the Dovre Mountains.»	Tell him: «To be sure, the cost in human toil and poverty and oppression has been great and besides it's nothing compared with the Holmenkollen Ski Jump or the Dovre Mountains.»

Defect	Possible Cause	Remedy
You have taken the Norwegian to the best luxury restaurant in your home town where the food is good, the wine excellent, and the chairs are comfortable to sit on. You have done this in order that he might enjoy himself and have a nice evening. But you can tell that he isn't enjoying himself and hasn't had a nice evening at all.	The Norwegian is sitting there, thinking: «What am I doing here? In all this luxury? I, a son of the Wilderness, who prefers simple things, for ex., like the *hytte*, where we sit on Norwegian stones and eat with our fingers right out of the fire.»	There is nothing you can do except pay the bill and, if possible, go somewhere else.
You ask the Norwegian to go to the right. He doesn't go to the right, but remains standing and declaims «Hamlet's Speech to the Actors» in English.	He is quite drunk, and hasn't understood what you asked him to do. (See: *The Norwegian and Intoxication*).	Give him a cup of coffee and try one more time.

These examples will apply in various ways if you want the Norwegian to sign other kinds of documents than fisheries agreements, or perform other acts than go to the right, left or straight ahead, for ex.: stand up, make love, sit down, open the door or pass the potatoes.

How to Aquire a Norwegian

If you are in the position that you do not have, have not met nor been in contact with a Norwegian, but would like to do so – even after reading the above – you should read the following:

Even though the Norwegian, for thousands of years, has lived more than a stone's throw from his closest neighbour, and is therefore unaccustomed to people other than his closest family, like most people he has *a social need*.

On certain occasions he likes to be with other people. But because he belongs to a pragmatic culture, and, thus, has a liking for the utilitarian *value* and *purpose* of things and actions, he would prefer that the time spent with other people be utilitarian and purposeful.

He wants the time he spends with other people to result in something sensible, or enable him to:

1. learn from it
2. have a child by it, or
3. obtain a good Fisheries Agreement.

The Norwegian has never quite understood how people from other lands can find it morally justifiable to sit in a pub, at a sidewalk cafe or in a marketplace for hours, and talk about anything for no other purpose than just sitting there talking.

In order to satisfy his social needs in a way that satisfies his desire for the expediency of his social needs, the Norwegian is a member of one or more *organizations*. In proportion to the population, no other country has as many organizations as Norway. In Norway there are almost as many organizations as there are inhabitants in the country:

Athletics organizations, fishing organizations, hunting organizations, hunting and fishing organizations, art organizations, organizations for combating smoking, organizations for the defense of organizations for combating smoking, organizations for combating organizations for the defense of organizations for combating smoking, etc., and organizations for the defense of the striped boring beetle.

To name a few.

When the Norwegian moves from one place to another, after a short time, he establishes an Organization for Outsiders from the Place He Comes From. This is also true when the Norwegian takes up residence, for shorter or longer periods, in another country.

Even if there is only one Norwegian living in your community, you may take it for granted that he has started an *Organization of Norwegians.*

In other words: If you would like to get to know the Norwegian, you can just go and say «Hello» to him in the Norwegians' Organization where you live. As a rule, the Norwegians' Organization has a meeting every Wednesday at 6 p.m., as well as every 17th of May.

Welcome and Good Luck.